WILD CATS

WILD CATS

CAROLINE BRETT

Photographs from the Bruce Coleman
Wildlife & Travel Photo Collection

B⬣XTREE

First published 1992 by
Boxtree Limited
36 Tavistock Street
London WC2E 7PB

Text © Caroline Brett

Edited by Miranda Smith
Designed by Sarah Hall

Colour reproduction by Fotographics Limited, Hong Kong
Typeset by Cambrian Typesetters, Frimley, Surrey
Printed and bound by Dai Nippon, Hong Kong

A CIP catalogue record for this book is available from the British Library

ISBN 1–85283–131–6

ACKNOWLEDGEMENTS

All pictures courtesy of Bruce Coleman Wildlife & Travel Photo Collection:
Jen and Des Bartlett 62, 82, 90, 114, 118; Erwin and Peggy Bauer 11, 39,
41 above, 51, 59, 63, 65, 86, 93, 104, 106, 107, 119; Mark N.
Boulton 66; Ron Cartmell 115; Bruce Coleman 43; Alain Compost 1,
40; Gerald Cubitt 47, 71, 96; Peter Davey 69 below, 78 below, 94, 98;
Francisco Erize 41 below, 68; P. Evans 2, 35; Jeff Foott 27; J. L. G.
Grande 49; Carol Hughes 111, 117; David Hughes 60; M. P. Kahl 77;
Stephen J. Krasemann 32, 72; Werner Layer 67; Mackinnon 80; Luiz
Claudio Marigo 15, 36, 54 above; Dr Norman Myers 95, 112, 113; Dieter
and Mary Plage 6, 36, 54 below, 87, 91, 102; G. D. Plage 48, 54 below;
M. P. Price 56; Hans Reinhard 19, 42, 46, 50, 75, 110; Leonard Lee Rue III
38, 69 above, 70, 73, 81, 85, 105, 116; John Shaw 17; A. J. Stevens 44; Rod
Williams 21, 37, 52, 55, 84 above and below, 89, 97; Joseph van Wormer 45;
Konrad Wothe 58, 64, 88, 92; Gunter Ziesler front jacket, back jackets, 23,
29, 53, 57, 74, 76, 79, 99, 100, 103, 108, 109, 118; J. P. Zwaenepoel
78 above

CONTENTS

INTRODUCTION

I have spent hours watching wild cats in zoos and wildlife parks, but still was not prepared for, nor did it compare with the magical experience of encountering a large cat in the wild. While looking for warthogs earlier this year, just after daybreak in Kenya's Nakuru National Park, I came across a huge male leopard. The unquestionable beauty of the animal sent shivers down my spine, and my arms developed a bad case of goose bumps. From the safety of my vehicle, I was able to watch and follow this incredible creature for several hours. While he totally ignored me, I was transfixed. It is an experience I will never forget and, as I left him sleeping peacefully sprawled on a branch of an acacia tree, I felt immensely privileged.

During the following week, I saw several more leopards and a pride of lions. Each encounter left me feeling overwhelmed not only by their grace and agility, but also by their power and an awareness of my own vulnerability. The awe and majesty of wild cats has inspired people for centuries and they continue to reign supreme among the world's most captivating animals.

CAROLINE BRETT

THE WILD CAT

THE EVOLUTION OF THE CAT

The first members of the cat family (the *Felidae*) appear in the fossil record thirty-five million years ago. Six million years later, the world was teeming with felids: lions, lynx and giant cheetahs roamed the forests of Europe, China and Asia.

About seventy million years ago, during the Eocene period, the world underwent an age of great change. The earth's crust was thinner than it is today and volcanic eruptions were a relatively frequent event. The exploding volcanoes shifted vast quantities of rock which resulted in the formation of mountains, seas and oceans, including the Atlantic and Indian Oceans. While glaciers flowed down the mountains, the climate on the plains was tropical and sustained flourishing forests, which in turn supported an abundance of rapidly evolving animals. Near the end of this period, during a burst of diversification, the first members of the family Carnivora, known as the Miacids, made an appearance. They were stoat-like in appearance with a long body and tail, short limbs and a small brain, but showed to some degree all the characteristics typical of modern carnivores, particularly in their dental arrangements. They also had large paws, supple toes and probably retractable claws, which enabled them to climb trees and grasp prey. One group of Miacids was destined to become the ancestors of bears, dogs, seals, pandas and all the members of the weasel family, while another gave rise to the cats, hyenas, genets, mongooses and civets.

During the Oligocene period, which followed on after the Eocene and lasted fifteen million years, the geological and climatic conditions on earth continued to change. Vast plains formed and the weather became more temperate, with hot summers and cool winters. This led to the diversification of grazing herbivores and in turn the carnivores which hunted them. It was during this period that *Dinictis*, the ancestor of all modern felids, as well as of the legendary sabre-toothed cats, evolved. Larger than Siberian tigers, which are the biggest of the present-day felids, the sabre-toothed cats were immensely powerful and distinctive for their outsized, blade-like upper canines. Equipped with fangs up to 15 cm (6 in) in length, they were able to dispatch with ease the huge lumbering herbivores which at that time wandered the plains.

While the sabre-toothed cats continued to dominate the feline niche during the Miocene period, which lasted for the next nineteen million years, ninety-five species of *Dinictis* evolved. Of these, thirty-eight exist in a recognizable form to this day.

One of the most successful was an animal which looked like a streamlined lynx. It had fully retractable claws which improved its hunting ability, giving it an advantage over other carnivores. Its claws no longer went blunt through general wear and tear and, although they were incredibly sharp, they could be tucked away out of harm's reach. With its claws sheathed, the animal could run fast without getting hooked up in tangled vegetation and also walk soundlessly over hard ground, since its claws no longer clicked and scraped on rocks. Yet, with its claws extended, each paw became a deadly weapon which was used like a grappling iron to grasp and hold onto prey. Its claws also enabled it to shin up trees, where it could both escape enemies and launch an aerial attack on unsuspecting victims.

As the world continued to change, so did the creatures which inhabited it. During the Pliocene period, which began eleven million years ago, the earth began to cool down and by the Pleistocene, a mere million years ago, the earth was experiencing an Ice Age. As the vast plains were increasingly ravaged by ice and snow, the giant herbivores died out and, as a consequence, so did the sabre-toothed cats. Only the fittest survived, but among those were thirty-eight species of supremely adapted carnivores, all members of the cat family.

EXTINCT WILD CATS

Today, all the existing members of the cat family are grouped together under the family *Felidae*. During the Miocene and Pliocene periods (between twenty-four and two million years ago), when the *Felidae* were evolving, the sabre-toothed cats dominated the feline niche.

Compared to modern cats, which have similar-sized canines in both their upper and lower jaws, the sabre-toothed cats had huge upper canines with tiny lower ones to make space for their massive counterparts. One species, called *Smilodon*, had long, conical canines designed for stabbing and piercing the throat of its prey. The upper canines of *Homotherium* were blade-like and equipped with serrated inner edges for severing the windpipe and jugular veins of its victims.

Modern day big cats, such as lions and tigers, often kill large victims with a fatal bite to the back of the neck which severs the spinal cord. Sabre-toothed cats probably never used this method as they could not afford to risk fracturing their huge but fragile canines on the vertebrae of their prey.

To use their elongated fangs effectively, sabre-toothed cats had to open their mouths into an exaggerated yawning gape which entailed throwing their heads back so far that they risked dislocating their necks. As a consequence, they developed enormous muscles at the front of their necks which supported their heads and backs during the deathblow.

With the gradual extinction of the giant herbivores, the sabre-toothed tigers also met their demise. They were too huge and bulky, their sickle-shaped teeth too long and they were too slow to catch smaller, swifter prey. So, after millions of successful years on earth, these giant cats become extinct.

CATS CLASSIFIED

There are big wild cats, small, striped, spotted, stocky and slender ones. Whatever their size, shape or colour, they all belong to that very uniform animal group, the *Felidae*. They can be recognized as cats, whether the animal is a weasel-like jaguarundi, a lithe cheetah or a maned lion. Since the sabre-toothed and false sabre-toothed cats are extinct, all existing members of the cat family or *Felidae* are now broken down into four groups or genera: *Acinonyx*, *Neofelis*, *Panthera* – the big cats, and *Felis* – the small cats.

Animals are grouped into species on their interbreeding abilities and whether they can produce fertile offspring. All types of domestic cat can freely intermate and produce viable offspring, so they belong to the same species. Tigers and lions do not mate with each other in the wild, but have been encouraged to do so in captivity. The offspring of the cross, called ligers and tigons, are either sterile or only weakly fertile, and therefore the tiger and lion are classified as separate species.

Currently, thirty-seven species of wild cat have been identified, but as scientists explore the world's last remote areas, new species may still be discovered. Only in 1965, the Japanese zoologist Imaizumi, found a small but distinctive dark brown, spotted cat with a unique skull and dental characteristics on the Japanese island of Ryukyu.

Cats are divided into groups or genera on basic structural characteristics. The cheetah, the sole member of the genus *Acinonyx*, has non-retractable claws.

ROARING CATS

The members of the genus *Panthera* – the lion, tiger, jaguar, leopard and snow leopard – are distinct in their ability to roar. This is thought to be due to the fact that the hyoid bone at the back of the throat has a cartilaginous section which permits greater freedom of movement, allowing sound to vibrate in the voice box, enabling these big cats to roar.

SMALL BUT DISTINCTIVE

In all other species of the *Felidae*, the hyoid consists entirely of bone which, while preventing them from roaring, allows them to purr, a noise the *Panthera* species are unable to make. The thirty-two species of 'small wild cats' differ from their larger relatives in several other ways. They feed lying alongside large prey rather than crouching over it, all have retractable claws, they generally spend more time grooming, and they have nose pads which are at least partly hairless, unlike the big cats which have completely furry noses.

The biggest small felid is the puma. Even though it is as large as a leopard, it has more characteristics in common with the smaller than the larger group. Small cats occur in all continents except Australia and Antarctica, their pupils are slit-shaped in bright light and their tails are banded.

CAT FACTS

The general assumption that all cats cannot sweat is untrue. They have well-developed sweat glands on their lips, chin, the area around the nipples and between the pads on their feet. Any cat owner who has taken their pet to the vet will have noticed wet paw prints on the surgery table. Cats, like most mammals, sweat when frightened.

Cat's teeth are designed for eating meat. Both the lower and upper jaw are equipped with small but razor-sharp cutting teeth and sword-shaped, powerful canines. The canines and incisors are used to grab and kill the prey; the small front teeth to scrape meat from bones, and in big cats to rip small pieces of flesh off a carcass; and the back teeth for cutting through pieces of meat. Their rough tongue is used in conjunction with their teeth and acts like a file. It enables them to clean bones by licking up the last traces of flesh.

After the teeth, the paws, armed with sharp, sickle-shaped claws, are the cat's most important weapon. They are usually retracted when the cat walks, and extended when the animal attacks. Retracted claws cannot usually be seen, since they fit inside claw sheaths. All cats walk on their toes but their weight is distributed on large sole pads, the 'balls of their feet', giving them graceful paces. They all have furred feet, but sand cats, lynx and snow leopards have extra hairy soles to protect them from baking sand or frozen ground.

SENSUAL CATS

As in all carnivores, wild cats have highly developed senses. Their perception of smell is good, but it is not as important as their vision or hearing. Cats rarely follow scent trails of prey. Their hearing is acute and their ears can accurately pin-point the slightest sound; this enables them to creep up and pounce on hidden prey. Their large eyes reflect how significant sight is to cats. They have binocular vision and see colour, but in dim light their eyes are about six times more sensitive than a human's and can adjust much more quickly to sudden darkness. A cell layer in the back of the eyeball reflects incidental light and enhances night vision. It makes a cat's eyes glow when caught in the headlights of a car. In addition to smell and taste, they have a third related sense, which utilizes the Jacobson's or vomeronasal organ, sited in the roof of the mouth. It is used to detect scent, mainly sex hormones in urine, by sucking in air behind their teeth and over the organ. The use of this organ is associated with the facial grimace or lip-curl known as the 'Flehman reaction', which is commonly seen during sexual encounters.

Cats also have exceptional balance and sense of equilibrium. This is a capability which is important, since the majority are forest-dwellers and climb trees. It is well known that if a cat is held upside-down by its legs and dropped, it will regain an upright position before hitting the floor, so long as it was held sufficiently high to give it time to turn over.

The cat's flexible whiskers, as well as the long, stiff hairs above the eyes and in the armpits, are highly touch sensitive. They help cats to find their way in the dark, which is important as many species hunt under the cover of darkness. Density of hair, colouring and patterning of coat vary considerably in relation to habitat. The basic colour is usually a shade of brown, grey, tawny or golden-yellow, and often patterned with darker stripes, rosettes or spots. Many species have a dark stripe – the tear stripe – running down their faces, from the corner of each eye.

HABITAT

Felids have penetrated almost every continental habitat, from rainforest to hot and cold deserts and mountain ranges. They are not found in treeless tundra areas, on polar ice and, apart from feral domestic cats, Australasia and some island groups. In many cases, species have adapted to suit the conditions in which they live. Tigers that are found in northern areas tend to be larger than the southern sub-species because a larger surface ratio loses a smaller proportion of body heat. They also have thicker coats for warmth. Black-coated cats such as the panther are found in forested areas where other predators and prey alike find it difficult to spot them.

Some species have become extinct or are endangered because of man's greed for land. The cats' habitat and food supplies have been exploited, and their exquisite fur coveted by the fashion-conscious. If people are not educated to realize that a cat's skin looks far better on the natural owner, we risk losing many of the most beautiful species forever.

OPPOSITE PAGE
The sandy-coloured caracal is a solitary hunter of dry grass lands, arid scrub and savannah, where its plain coat matches perfectly with the buff-coloured vegetation and soil.

WARNING OFF INTRUDERS

The great majority of wild cats lead solitary lives. Most of them form temporary bonds only during the breeding season, when pairs may hunt together and when females are accompanied by dependent young. Lions are exceptions, since they live and hunt as family groups. The Indian tiger is also occasionally a social hunter.

Since most cats are loners, each animal occupies its own territory. A territory contains specific sites for sleeping, resting, patrolling and marking. The cats mark their boundaries by scratching trees, defecating and urinating on prominent landmarks like stumps and boulders. These signals inform competitors that the area is occupied and warns them to 'keep out'. This natural behaviour can be irritating for domestic cat owners, when furniture is substituted for a tree trunk or a 'tom' leaves his 'calling card'. Males generally have larger territories than females and several territories can overlap. Outside the mating season, individuals of the same species generally give each other a wide berth: combats can be fatal and are best avoided. The core and breeding areas are strongly defended but fights only usually break out between males competing for a female.

CAT HUNT

More carnivorous than any other carnivore, wild cats are supreme hunters among terrestrial mammals with virtually no enemies other than man. Unlike the dog family, most felids are solitary hunters incapable of a long-distance chase.

Except for lions, they do not hunt as a unit, like wolves or African hunting dogs; instead they lie in wait, creep up on, ambush or sprint after prey. Felids approach their prey in a low, creeping run that is often interrupted by pauses. The final pounce occurs from a close distance. The hind legs remain on the ground until the cat has caught its victim, grabbing it with its forepaws. The cat can then adjust for escape manoeuvres or changes in the course of its prey. Just a few species, like the clouded leopard and the margay, jump on their victims from above without first landing on the ground. Fleeing animals can be pursued at top speed but only in short bursts.

Although they have a reputation for wanton slaughter, only well-fed domestic cats play 'the cat and mouse game' and kill more than they need to eat. Wild cats spend a great deal of time just finding potential prey. They often have to walk many kilometres or lie in wait for hours. Even then, they are frequently unsuccessful in making a kill. Their normal behaviour is only thrown off-balance when they encounter an unnatural situation, most commonly where domestic stock are confined in a small area.

CAT FOOD

A cat's diet consists almost exclusively of meat. They prey on vertebrates (animals with backbones), ranging from mammals the size of zebra to mice, large and small birds, fish, reptiles and amphibians. Invertebrates (animals without backbones), mainly insects and crustaceans, are also included in the diet of some species. Cats sometimes eat grass, a habit well-

known to all cat-owners, although this is not generally associated with nutritional requirements. When a cat grooms, it often swallows a large amount of loose hair which mats together in its stomach. Grass and other plant material are thought to help get rid of 'fur balls', either by easing their passage through their gut or by helping the cat to cough up the furry obstruction.

FAMILY CATS

Most male and female cats bear a strong resemblance to each other, although males are usually larger, have thicker heads and are heavier than females. The lion is the only wild cat with pronounced sexual differences, since only the male has a mane. The marking of young cats differ from the adult coloration in some species. For example, lion cubs have spots; young pumas are usually red-brown or cinnamon and always have large, blackish blotches, while the adult coat is uniform; newborn cheetahs have a long, white-grey mane extending across the neck and back, while the parents have short hair all over their bodies.

During the breeding period, both sexes wander more than usual, thereby increasing their chances of finding a mate. Females coming into season are often very vocal, calling frequently to attract any males in the vicinity. Fights between males can be violent. The female often sits at a disinterested distance to await the outcome. The victor usually asserts his authority by stalking about and scent-marking. By the time he returns, the female may have gone off with the loser – she does not invariably form a pair bond with the winner!

When a male and female first meet, they circle each other, testing the other's state of receptiveness. The formalities over, they often roll provocatively but do not mate until they are better acquainted. Males court by uttering specific calls and usually initiate sexual advances, but as the female comes more into heat, she plays an increasingly active role. Only when she is ready, after much head and body rubbing, does copulation occur. Mating lasts a few minutes with the male grabbing the female's nape as he ejaculates, and often ends with the female turning on her partner, hissing and striking out at him.

Females bear between one and six young usually once a year when prey is most abundant, which varies according to habitat. Large wild cats do not usually mate again for two years, since their offspring are dependent on their mother for

at least eighteen months. Some species, such as the Siberian tiger, only give birth to one cub every three to four years.

Kittens are born blind and helpless. Their mother often builds a nest, since they require protection from wind, rain and cold. In most species, the male leaves soon after mating to seek a new partner, and the female raises the young alone. Young cats learn to recognize prey by the food their mother brings to them. Later, by playing with live prey and accompanying their mother, they learn to develop their natural hunting instincts and to make use of the experience to become efficient predators.

BLACK CATS AND WHITE CATS

Several species of wild cat have a black or melanistic variety. Melanism is a common coat colour mutation, probably caused by a recessive gene, and has been recorded in jaguars, tigers, lions, leopards, mountain lions, caracals, bobcats, margays, ocelots and servals. Black jaguars and leopards which have both been described as black panthers, are most common in the jungle. So little light penetrates the forest canopy that a dark-coloured coat is an advantage for concealment.

Leucism, or the lack of dark pigmentation, also occurs quite widely in different cat species. The most famous are the white tigers of Rewa, now selectively bred in zoos, and the white lions of Timbavati.

THE ULTIMATE CARNIVORE

Cats are equipped with everything that a supreme hunter needs: ultra-efficient ears, eyes and whiskers to pin-point the exact position of prey; camouflaged coats which enable them to melt into their surroundings; a weaponry of sharp claws and teeth; agile and athletic bodies; and a fine-tuned sense of balance and orientation. They are also the most magnificent, dignified and beautiful family of mammals.

SPOTTED CATS

Spots are the ultimate in disruptive camouflage. They perfectly mimic the dappling of light and shade in the forest or in the patches of bush where spotted cats spend most of their lives hunting, eating, caring for their young and sleeping.

JAGUAR

Panthera onca

The American continents are the exclusive domain of one of the big cats – the jaguar. Unlike its large relatives, it does not often roar, a characteristic it shares with the snow leopard. Although it is less vocal than other big cats, it grunts while hunting, mews during courtship, and growls when threatened.

It looks similar to the leopard but is, in comparison, a muscular bruiser, having a heavier build and a more massive, rounded head. It is most easily distinguished by the dots in the middle of the rosette patterns which mark its pelt. The base colour of its body can be any shade of yellow through to tawny-red. Its markings are very variable and often merge into stripes along its spine. Melanistic, or black, animals are common in zoos as a result of selective breeding, but they occur only occasionally in the wild.

Jaguars are found from the southern states of North America, where they are extremely rare, through Central and South America to southern Brazil. They prefer dense forest, and open savannah with good cover and easy access to water, although they will hunt in more open country when necessary. They swim and climb well, and usually hunt between dawn and dusk from the ground. Prey species include deer, tapir, large and small rodents, sloths, monkeys, caiman, and turtles and their eggs. They will also take domestic cattle and horses where they are easily available.

Jaguars, like tigers, have no fear of water. They often lie near the river's edge twitching their tail from side to side much like an irritated domestic cat. This habit has led local Amerindians to believe that jaguars use their tails as fishing rods, the tips acting as lures to tempt fish within their grasp. *Characteristics: length of head and body 1.8 m (6 ft), tail 56 cm (22 in), weight 41–136 kg (90–300 lb)*

LEOPARD

Panthera pardus

The leopard is smaller than the jaguar but a powerful animal even so. It is a stocky, muscular cat with a strong neck and head. Like an alley-cat, it is a creature of shadow and shade. It is also a loner. Except for mating pairs and females with cubs, the leopard always leads a solitary existence. Its camouflage of striking black rosettes and spots on a straw-coloured coat, originally developed for the forests, is still effective in savannah and bush land because it is a constant seeker of cover and seclusion.

Leopards were once thought to be a cross between a lion (*Leo*) and a 'pard' or panther, hence their name. A hundred years ago, the fabled 'black panther' was believed to be a separate species which included the melanistic form of the leopard, jaguar and serval. It is now known that black cats are simply colour variants. To add to the confusion, the words 'pard' and panther have also been used to describe jaguars and pumas.

The leopard is the most widely distributed of all the big cats because it is one of the most adaptive. Its range includes desert and rainforest, mountains and coastal plains, in both Africa and South East Asia. It is an opportunistic hunter and unlike many other large carnivores feeds on both large and small prey.

A large part of the leopard's diet is made up of rodents and birds, but it is also capable of killing much bigger prey. A single leopard has been known to bring down a full-grown bull eland, weighing over 454 kg (1,000 lb), and even a male gorilla was once killed by a leopard which was only a quarter of the ape's weight. The leopard hunts by stalking, relying on its spots as camouflage, then making a short, swift charge. The kill is made with a deep, penetrating bite to the base of the skull or a throat bite.

With its hooked claws and compact, muscular build, the leopard is a natural climber, which is important for safety as well as hunting efficiency. It can escape up a tree when threatened by a pride of hungry lions which are less agile and poor climbers. An antelope carcass can last a leopard five to six days but only if it can hang on to it. An adult leopard can carry its own weight and more, high into the branches, and by hauling its catch aloft, it can cache it safely out of the reach of lions, hyenas, jackals and vultures.

Capable of feeding on almost anything, and hiding almost anywhere, the leopard is even found on the outskirts of large cities like the forested suburbs of Nairobi. It has been known

OPPOSITE PAGE
Jaguars, like other big cats, have an exceptional sense of balance, something which is vital for their arboreal way of life.

for leopards to use swimming-pools as watering-holes and any dogs allowed to roam at night are regarded as fair game.

Characteristics: length of head and body about 122 cm (48 in), tail 61 cm (24 in), weight 32–54 kg (70–120 lb)

SNOW LEOPARD
Panthera uncia

Often called the ounce, this shy, elusive and little studied cat has a dense, woolly, smoky-grey coat which is tinged with yellow on its flanks, pale underneath with blurred rosettes on its body and rows of black spots on its head. It is grouped among the big cats, but it also shares several characteristics with its smaller relatives: for example, it feeds crouched alongside rather than standing over or sprawled on top of its prey. It does not often roar, but several observers report that it can – and loudly.

Its coat was highly valued by the fur trade and years of persecution have led to its near extinction. Today, it only survives in high mountains above the tree line in Kashmir, Tibet, Ladkh and the Himalayas where it hunts ground birds and mammals ranging from ibex, wild sheep and boar to marmots and mice. Since prey in this rarefied atmosphere are thin on the ground, the cat's territory is correspondingly large, up to 100 square kilometres (40 square miles). It is, however, well adapted for life at high altitudes with its thick, insulating coat to keep it warm during the cold months. The soles of its paws are furry and this protects the naked pads from the cold. Its wide paws act as snow shoes, distributing the weight of the animal evenly on soft snow.

Characteristics: length of head and body 104 cm (41 in), tail 89 cm (35 in), weight 45–68 kg (100–150 lb)

CHEETAH
Acinonyx jabatus

The cheetah is widespread, and can be found in both Africa and Asia. A slender, almost fragile animal, it is a creature of the open plains. It is the fastest animal on land and can sprint at up to 96 kph (60 mph) for a brief part of its chase. It has a long, heavy-tipped tail, that helps to balance it during its high-speed runs; small, uniformly-sized spots; a small head, with clamp-like jaws; short whiskers and a tear-stained face.

Unlike other cats, the cheetah's claws when retracted are not covered by a sheath, but are left exposed to provide additional traction during rapid acceleration. On the outside of its wrist, a sharp dew-claw is used like a grappling iron to trip its prey. Its very long legs and elongated, flexible spine give it great sprinting prowess but it lacks endurance. This means it can only hunt effectively in open country where there is sufficient cover for stalking. The cheetah's jaws are not very powerful. They cannot break an animal's neck, like a jaguar or leopard, in fact they seldom even break the skin of their prey in a kill.

After a high-speed chase, the cheetah's quarry is exhausted and totally out of breath. By encasing the nose and mouth of its prey in its own jaws or by grasping its throat, the cat clamps off the air supply and its victim rapidly suffocates. The cheetah concentrates on small antelope and in particular the Thompson's gazelle. Not only is the cheetah fussy about the type of food it eats, but also the way it gets it. Unlike leopards, which will scavenge a stinking carcass, or lions which regularly steal from other carnivores, the cheetah will only eat what it has killed itself. Unlike the leopard, it cannot haul its prey up into a tree. Instead it drags it under any available cover and eats as fast as it can in order to swallow as much as possible before the scavengers move in. Vultures are the bane of a cheetah's life. Soaring high above the plains, they spot potential food from miles around and can 'drop in' on a kill, often within minutes. As the vultures descend, they alert lions and hyenas and, before long, they too are in on the action. Unable to defend its catch against such powerful adversaries, the cheetah is then forced into deserting its meal.

In the wet months from November to May, the Thompson's gazelles move away from the woodlands out into the open plains – and the cheetahs follow them. During this period of plenty, female cheetahs set up overlapping home ranges of up to 775 sq. km (300 sq. miles) which contain all they need to raise their young – cover and plenty of food.

A cheetah bears up to six cubs, which have a mantle of grey fur that they lose at about four months. Mortality is high; by three months, ninety per cent of the cubs will die, victims of lions, hyenas, bush fires and hunger. But if all the cubs survived, the African plains would be over-run with cheetahs. The surviving youngsters stay with their mothers for up to eighteen months. Young females then go it alone, but the male cubs stay together, in a coalition that often lasts for life. This is because in order to get access to females, the males have to mark out and hold a territory. A group of males is

*Many of the spotted cats, like the ocelot, are now
endangered, as their pelts are the most highly coveted by people
for making fur coats. The ocelot became a fully protected
species in 1975, but it is still killed as a pest, and its kittens sold
as pets in Central and South America.*

much more successful than a single animal but being one of a crowd means having to share potential mates. At least by joining forces, they have access to more females, so the individual's chances of mating are increased. Solitary male cheetahs are rarely able to hold a territory of their own. They are usually in poor condition, and lead frustrated lives, lying low to avoid large predators, especially groups of male cheetahs, who can wound them fatally if they get into a fight.

When a female comes into season, it is also easier for a group of males to follow her until she comes into oestrus. Until that time, females do their best to shake off any suitors and one is easier to evade than three. A group of males can stick with her for days, taking it in turns to sleep and feed until she is finally in a receptive mood. Then, they will probably all mate with her, but even if only one does, since they are all brothers, genetically it will be a success. As siblings, they share 50 per cent of their genes and if one helps another to mate, it ensures that the breeding line is successfully continued.

Up to six sub-species of cheetah have been described, but most scientists think they should all be classified as one species. Even the Asian cheetah may not be a valid race and the fabled king cheetah, which was described as a new species, simply has a single genetic mutation which causes it to have a blotched rather than spotted coat.

Characteristics: length of head and body 1.2–1.5 m (4–5 ft), tail 50–76 cm (20–30 in), weight 38–63 kg (85–140 lb)

NORTHERN LYNX
Felis lynx

This powerful and sturdily built cat has a distinctive, short tail and tufted ears. Its coat is yellow-brown and usually marked with darker spots. It is found in North America and from Europe to Siberia where it lives in pine forests and thick scrub, hunting rodents, birds, fish, deer and sheep mainly at night.

The lynx is one of the three main species of wild cat which inhabits North America. The availability of its main prey in this continent, the snowshoe hare, appears to determine its range and spatial organization. Where hares are abundant males tend to range over an area of 50 sq. km (19 sq. miles), but when hare populations crash, a periodic occurrence in the north, home ranges enlarge, and there is more overlapping as individuals compete for the remaining populations of their prey. When the number of hares declines dramatically, lynx have been known to travel over 480 km (300 miles) in search of something to eat.

Characteristics: length of head and body 102 cm (40 in), tail 18 cm (7 in), weight 14–29 kg (30–65 lb)

SPANISH LYNX
Felis pardina

This beautiful cat is slightly smaller than its northern relative and its large round paws grow thick pads of hair in winter. It is only found in the Iberian peninsula where it is nocturnal and preys on rodents, birds, fish, insects and the occasional deer and sheep.

Characteristics: length of head and body 96 cm (38 in), tail 13 cm (5 in), weight 24 kg (54 lb)

OCELOT
Felis pardalis

One of the most beautiful of all cats, the ocelot has been driven to the point of extinction by the demand for its pelt. No two individual animals look exactly alike but the oblique, elongated spots are generally black with a slightly paler centre, on a pale yellow background. The ocelot's head is boldly marked with solid black spots and cheek lines, its tail is either ringed or barred and its rounded black-backed ears have central yellow spots. It ranges from the southern states of North America to central South America. It is found in a variety of habitats from dense humid jungle to thorny scrub, but never out in the open. It is generally nocturnal and terrestrial, but rests during the day in high trees. It is highly territorial and preys on birds, deer, peccaries, coatimundi and agouti.

Characteristics: length of head and body 89 cm (35 in), tail 41 cm (16 in), weight 5.4–13.6 kg (12–30 lb)

OPPOSITE PAGE
The North American lynx generally prefers forested regions, but they are found in more open areas, and even farmland, if it is interspersed with thickly wooded terrain. Historically, the cat was widely distributed in North America but, due to the demand for its pelt, it is now confined to Canada and Alaska.

SERVAL
Felis serval

The serval is about the size of an alsatian dog but is longer legged and more sinuous. Its most noticeable feature is its huge ears. They swivel and search like radar dishes, and can locate a mouse 6 m (20 ft) away. It then uses its long legs to run towards and spring on prey, pinning it to the ground with its forefeet.

Under its spots, the serval is a pale buff or reddish yellow. It has a spotted tail with a black tip and the backs of its ears are black with distinctive white spots. It is found in Algeria and Africa south of the Sahara, and always near water with dense cover, such as reed beds, high grass or scrub. It is nocturnal, but a hungry serval will also hunt during the day, searching for any lizards, small rodents, birds and ungulates that it can find.
Characteristics: length of head and body 81 cm (32 in), tail 41 cm (16 in), weight 16 kg (35 lb)

FISHING CAT
Felis viverrinus

The fishing cat is heavily built with dark, brown spots running in longitudinal rows on a coarse grey coat. It has distinctive white spots on its round ears and partially webbed paws. It is active during the day and feeds on frogs, snakes, small mammals and birds in swamps and marshes in southern and south eastern Asia.
Characteristics: length of head and body 81 cm (32 in), tail 30 cm (12 in), weight 11.3 kg (25 lb)

MARGAY
Felis wiedii

Often called the 'little ocelot', or marguey, the name margay is translated more literally as 'tiger cat'. It is slim in build with long legs and tail, marked with dark spots and blotches which join to form bars down the back of its head and neck. This Central and South American forest dweller is mainly diurnal and arboreal, and it hunts birds, tree frogs, lizards and small mammals.
Characteristics: length of head and body 66 cm (26 in), tail 41 cm (16 in), weight 4–8.1 kg (9–18 lb)

LEOPARD CAT
Felis bengalensis

This species varies in colour from grey to red, with white underparts and dark spots all over the body except the head, which is boldly striped with black and white markings. It is found in forest regions from Kashmir east to Siberia, China and the Philippines. The leopard cat is arboreal and hunts game birds, small mammals and fish.
Characteristics: length of head and body 63–81 cm (25–32 in), tail 25–35 cm (10–14 in), weight 3–7 kg (7–15 lb)

IRIOMOTE CAT
Felis iriomotensis

Discovered in 1965, this cat is confined to the 292 sq. km (113 sq. miles) island of Iriomotejima in the Yaeyama Islands, which lie off the Ryukyu group running to the south of Japan. Little is known about this species, but it is thought that fewer than 100 animals survive, due to the destruction of the sub-tropical rainforest where they live, and which once covered several islands. The Iriomote cat is similar to the leopard cat, has short legs and tail, a long body, and dark spots which may coalesce into bands which pattern its brown coat. Dark stripes run along its neck, and the ears are dark with central white spots.
Characteristics: length of head and body 51–56 cm (20–22 in), tail 20–30 cm (8–12 in), weight 3.2–4.1 kg (7–9 lb)

TIGER CAT
Felis tigrina

Sometimes called the little spotted cat, or oncilla, the tiger cat is very similar to the margay, but has slightly smaller spots and a rougher coat texture. It also lives in Central and South America where it is a typical arboreal, forest dweller, hunting small birds and rodents from dawn until dusk.
Characteristics: length of head and body 56 cm (22 in), tail 33 cm (13 in), weight 2.2–3.6 kg (5–8 lb)

OPPOSITE PAGE
Servals hunt rodents and birds in long grass principally by sound rather than sight. Their huge ears swivel like radar dishes and pin-point the position of unseen prey.

GEOFFROY'S CAT

Felis geoffroyi

Named after Geoffroy St Hilaire, the French naturalist, this striking little cat is known as 'gato montes', or the mountain cat, in Argentina. In various shades of ochre to silver grey, its coat is covered with equally spaced, small, black spots which sometimes merge into bars on the forelegs and flanks. There are large white spots on the back of its ears. This South American cat hunts small mammals and birds mainly at night, in open bush and scrubby woodlands.

Characteristics: length of head and body 51 cm (20 in), tail 30 cm (12 in), weight 2.7 kg (6 lb)

KODKOD

Felis guigna

Probably the smallest wild cat in the western hemisphere, the kodkod's coat is buff-coloured with heavy round black spots, the tail is ringed and its ears have black backs with white central spots. It is a South America forest dweller which preys on small birds and mammals at night. Although it is an expert climber, it prefers to hunt at ground level.

Characteristics: length of head and body 46 cm (18 in), tail 20 cm (8 in), weight about 2 kg (4 lb)

STRIPED CATS

Stripes are the perfect camouflage for cats which live in tall grass and jungles where the shadows are more linear. The stripes disrupt the animal's outline as it stalks or lies in ambush for prey, enabling it to blend in with its background.

TIGER

Panthera tigris

For centuries, the tiger has been regarded with great respect and awe, no doubt partly due to the fact that it is a renowned man-eater. This magnificent beast has inspired numerous artists, writers and poets, including William Blake, who wrote the poem 'Tyger Tyger burning bright'. It also had the misfortune to be regarded as royal game and was hunted by kings.

The tiger ranges from India to Siberia and South East Asia. There are seven sub-species: the Siberian, the South China, the Indochina, the Bengal, the Sumatran, the Javan and the Caspian tiger. The tiger's coat may be any shade from pale cream to tawny, with vertical stripes of grey, brown or black, and no two tigers have identical markings. Its round ears have black backs with distinctive, central white spots. Although tigers look similar there are characteristic regional differences. The Siberian tiger is the largest and generally has the palest coat, while the Indo-Chinese sub-species is the smallest and darkest. The size and number of their stripes differ too. The Chinese tiger has the fewest stripes and the Sumatran the most. The latter also has a pronounced ruff.

The tiger, like all big cats, is designed for tackling large prey with its heavy build and muscular body providing great strength and weight. Its hind legs are longer than its forelimbs, and used for rapid acceleration and to spring on to the back of its victims. Its paws are equipped with large, sharp, retractable claws which are used for grasping and pinning down prey. The quarry is dispatched with a bite to the back of the neck or with a suffocating throat hold.

The Indian tiger is occasionally a social and diurnal hunter, but the other sub-species are predominantly solitary and nocturnal. They are wide-ranging but rarely found in open habitats. Their bold stripes make them conspicuous in flat terrain and so are most at home in dense forests where a background of dappled light and linear shadows are the perfect camouflage. They use all available cover to stalk or ambush prey like large deer, and they feed on a great variety of game from ungulates and primates to domestic stock, and occasionally termites, frogs and birds.

Tigers are basically solitary, although from the age of sexual maturity, females usually have cubs in tow. Since tigers can capture prey single-handedly, there is no advantage for the species to hunt in co-ordinated groups, and this explains why they are loners. However, they are not anti-social cats, occasionally sharing a kill where prey is plentiful in the wild, and living together harmoniously in zoos.

Characteristics: length of head and body 1.5–1.8 m (5–6 ft), tail 0.6–0.9 m (2–3 ft), weight 113–227 kg (250–500 lb)

OPPOSITE PAGE

The tiger's striped coat breaks up its outline and helps it stalk prey without being seen. When it is within 10–20 m (33–40 ft) of a potential victim, it bursts from cover.

THE SIBERIAN TIGER
Panthera tigris altaica

The Siberian tiger is a sub-species and the largest living felid. It is a tremendously powerful animal, heavier in the head and fore-quarters than any other cat and with longer hair than other tigers. It was once much more widely distributed, but today it only survives in a few isolated Amur-Ussuri regions in Siberia, and possibly in north-eastern China and north Korea. No one knows how many survive in the wild, but it is probably no more than a few hundred. Efforts to save these tigers have been made in Russia; they were given legal protection in 1948 and the wild ungulates on which they prey have also been protected in an attempt to reduce predation on domestic stock.
Characteristics: length of head and body up to 2.8 m (9 ft), tail up to 95 cm (37 in), weight up to 300 kg (661 lb)

WILD CAT
Felis silvestris

The wild cat is one of the most widely distributed of the small cats and is found in several different habitats. Its coat colour varies with location to aid concealment. The differences have led to the species being further divided into three sub-species, although not all scientists agree on this issue.
Characteristics: length of head and body 50–80 cm (19–31 in), tail up to 95 cm (37 in), weight 3–8 kg (7–30 lb)

EUROPEAN WILD CAT
Felis silvestris silvestris

A sub-species of the wild cat and about one-third bigger than the domestic cat, the European wild cat is sturdily built with long legs. This amber-eyed tabby cat has four or five stripes running from its forehead and down the back of its neck until they merge into a dorsal line which runs to the root of the tail. From this stripe, dark bands run down the body in solid or broken bars. The tail is banded, ending in a dark tip. The cat is found in Europe and western Asia in high woodlands, rocky terrain and occasionally on heaths, moors and marshes where food is abundant. It hunts, mainly at dawn and dusk, for small rodents, birds, squirrels and fawns.
Characteristics: length of head and body 56–71 cm (22–28 in), tail 30 cm (12 in), weight 4.5–13.6 kg (10–30 lb)

AFRICAN WILD CAT
Felis silvestris libyca

The African wild cat is a sub-species and an ancestor of the domestic cat. It is a little larger and stockier than its tame descendant. A tabby-sized, tabby-coloured creature, it lives on mice and lizards on the open plains. Smaller than the golden cat, it is similar in habits and colouring except for its tabby markings. Like many striped cats, it has the vestigial spotting on its flanks, a remnant of its forest-dwelling ancestors.

It lives in all types of country in Africa and Eurasia; and hunts small mammals, lizards, insects and birds, hunting mainly on the ground and at night.
Characteristics: length of head and body 50 cm (19 in), tail 30 cm (12 in), weight 4.5–8.1 kg (10–18 lb)

INDIAN DESERT CAT
Felis silvestris ornata

The Indian desert or steppe cat is adapted to the semi-deserts and steppes of south-western Asia as far east as India. It differs from the other wild cat sub-species by being a pale sandy or grey colour with distinctive black spots. It is thought that the Indian desert cat is an ancestor of Asian breeds of the domestic cat.
Characteristics: length of head and body 40–48 cm (16–19 in), tail 25 cm (10 in), weight 3.2 kg (7 lb)

PAMPAS CAT
Felis colocolo

About the size of a domestic cat, the pampas cat is known as 'gato pajero' or the 'grass cat', in Argentina. It has a broad face, pointed ears, and a coat which varies from pale, silvery grey through all tones of yellow to brown. Its sides, bushy tail and legs are banded with dark yellow or brown.

The pampas cat lives in South America on open grassland and high pampas, where it hunts birds and small mammals, particularly cavies, which are the wild ancestors of our domestic guinea-pigs.
Characteristics: length of head and body 61 cm (24 in), tail 30 cm (12 in), weight 3.6–6.3 kg (8–14 lb)

SPOTS AND STRIPES

CLOUDED LEOPARD
Neofelis nebulosa

This stunningly beautiful cat is called the mint leopard in China because its markings are shaped like the leaves of the mint that grows locally. Its coat varies from pale to rich brown and is distinctively patterned with black stripes, spots and blotches. The clouded leopard, like the snow leopard, cannot be conveniently placed within either the big or small cats categories since it shares characteristics common to both groups. For instance, it cannot roar because it has a rigid hyoid bone. The clouded leopard lives in the forests of southern Asia, Borneo and Sumatra. It is a predominantly arboreal species, most active at dawn and dusk, and preys on mammals, including monkeys and squirrels as well as various birds and reptiles. It is an agile, athletic climber, can descend tree trunks headfirst, crawl 'sloth-like' upside down along the undersides of branches and is one of the few cats which launches itself onto prey from an overhanging branch.
Characteristics: length of head and body 91 cm (36 in), tail 76 cm (30 in), weight 21.7 kg (48 lb)

BOBCAT
Felis rufus

Occasionally called the bay lynx, the bobcat is smaller and more slender than the northern lynx. Its ears are pointed and sometimes tufted, and its buff coat is spotted and barred with dark brown or black markings. There are eleven sub-species which range from British Columbia, south and east to central Mexico. The cat inhabits chaparral, semi-desert, brush, woodlands, swamp forest and open terrain. Small mammals are its main prey but it also kills birds and weak or sickly ungulates, and scavenges on deer carcasses in winter.
Characteristics: length of head and body 76 cm (30 in), tail 15 cm (6 in), weight 6.8–15.8 kg (15–35 lb)

MOUNTAIN CAT
Felis jacobita

As its name suggests, the mountain cat lives in mountainous zones, sometimes above the snow line, in southern Peru, northern Chile and north west Argentina. It is also called the Andean highland cat. The hairs of its exceptionally soft, fine coat are often over 5 cm (2 in) long, and pale silver in colour with darker markings of brown or orange on its body, graduating to black on its underparts and legs. Little is known about this cat but it is believed to be mainly diurnal and hunt small rodents such as chinchilla and viscacha.
Characteristics: length of head and body 58 cm (23 in), tail 36 cm (14 in), weight 3.6–6.8 kg (8–15 lb).

MARBLED CAT
Felis marmorata

This beautifully coloured cat is similar in colouring to the clouded leopard, with dark spots outlined sharply in black against a paler background. It is an arboreal forest-dweller which hunts birds during the day and lives in southern Asia, Sumatra and Borneo.
Characteristics: length of head and body 53 cm (21 in), tail 38 cm (15 in), weight 5.4 kg (12 lb)

A COAT OF ONE COLOUR

As prey species moved out on the plains, their predators, including several species of wild cat, followed them. Stripes and spots which had been the perfect camouflage in the forest made them highly visible under the bright sunlight of flat open expanses. Gradually, they lost their markings and the cats developed a uniform coat of one colour.

LION
Panthera leo

Its great size, strength and hunting prowess, has earned the lion the title of 'king of the beasts'. Until recently, it was believed to have supernatural powers which could be transferred to any warrior who ate or wore parts of this large cat. These powers included the gift of long life, a cure to illness and revived vigour. A few trophy hunters still regard the lion as an ultimate quarry. The fearsome image associated with this cat gives these people the chance to show off their courage and skill. In recent times, public opinion has changed and hunters are being replaced by tourists whose sights are now set through the lens of a camera or camcorder.

Lions are the colour of dry grass, but their bellies and

flanks, especially of the cubs, are clearly marked with spots – a reminder of their origins in the more forested past.

They inhabit Africa south of the Sahara Desert and their range extends from semi-deserts to open woodland and savannah, but they are most at home on open, grassy plains. They hunt both during the day and at night, mainly on large ungulates. However, they are also opportunistic feeders known to eat rodents, birds, reptiles and carrion.

Males are considerably larger than females and have a distinctive mane. Their greater size gives them considerable advantage at a kill, where they are able to crowd in and steal the carcass for themselves. Males rarely participate in hunts since they are slower and more visible. Instead, they often survive exclusively on kills made by the pride lionesses. The male's chief role is to defend their territory and family from rival males, and size is an obvious advantage. Their mane gives an illusion of great size without the drawback of increased weight. Confrontations between males are rare and the smaller animal usually withdraws before it comes to blows, but when fights do occur, the mane also acts as a protective shield against the opponent's teeth and claws.

The lion's cryptic coloration camouflages it out on the open plains, and helps it to get within close proximity of its quarry in order to make a successful kill. Prey species like wildebeest and zebra keep a constant look-out for any unusual movement and often detect even the most stealthy approach of a stalking lion before it is within range. To overcome this problem, lions often rely on teamwork to ambush a chosen victim and drive it within the range of a hidden member of the group.

The requirement to hunt together has necessitated the need to live together and, as a result, lions have evolved into the most social of all felids. They live in groups called prides, which usually include between four and twelve related lionesses, their cubs, and one to four unrelated males. As young males reach sexual maturity, they are expelled from their maternal pride by the dominant adult males. They usually leave with brothers or cousins of the same age, and often remain together for the rest of their lives. During their adolescent years, they become close companions, which is a considerable advantage when the time comes for them to take over an established pride from resident males past their physical peak. By joining forces, a group of young males can overpower a partnership of older males, particularly if they have lost a male relative through natural causes.

Even though males fight fiercely and cooperatively together against rivals, they do not compete over receptive females. Since they rely on each other to maintain control of the pride and are capable of inflicting serious wounds, fighting would only weaken their coalition. Instead, when a pride female comes into heat, they operate a kind of gentlemen's agreement on a first come first served basis. If a male allows a related companion to mate with one of the lionesses, some of his own genes will still be passed on to the cubs.

Although established male lions are extremely tolerant of their own young, when a new group takes over a pride, they often kill all the existing young cubs in what appears to be a gruesome massacre. But when a lactating female loses her offspring, she soon comes back into season and within days will be ready to mate with the slayer of her last litter. By killing another male's offspring, the incumbents increase the number of young they can themselves father. This is important since they never know how long their reign will last. Their own cubs will also survive better if there are no older cubs to compete with them.
Characteristics: length of head and body 2.4–2.7 m (8–9 ft), tail 0.6–0.9 m (2–3 ft), weight 136–181 kg (300–400 lb)

ASIAN LION
Panthera leo persica

Asian lions once roamed through Europe and Asia eastwards to northern India. Due to the activities of people, their numbers and range have declined dramatically over the last two hundred years. Today, all that remains of this sub-species is one small group containing only a few hundred in the Gir Forest in north-west India. Asian lions have a thicker coat, a longer tail tassel, a more pronounced belly fringe and a smaller mane than their African relatives. They also have hairy elbows and are stockier in build. Hunting mainly during the day, they frequent open, dry scrub country.
Characteristics: length of head and body 2.4–2.7 m (8–9 ft), tail 0.6–0.9 m (2–3 ft), weight 136–181 kg (300–400 lb)

OPPOSITE PAGE
Pumas have a fierce reputation that is undeserved. They do occasionally kill domestic stock and pet dogs, but there are few authenticated reports of attacks on humans. Pumas are shy and retiring by nature, and generally try to avoid all contact with people.

PUMA
Felis concolor

The most widespread of all the American cats, the puma, varies greatly in size and weight. The name 'puma' means 'large cat' in the Quechua language of Peru. Pioneer settlers gave this cat many other names, including cougar, mountain lion, panther, brown tiger and king cat. It has a neat, blunt head, small round ears, a lithe body and strong, muscular legs. Its hind limbs, which are longer than its forelegs, give it an elevated rump. There are two colour phases. The grey ranges from silver through to dark slate, and the red from pale buff to dark, fox red. The red phase cats are generally found in tropical areas, while the grey ones inhabit temperate forests. Both types intermate freely, and mixed litters are not uncommon. Young pumas are distinctly spotted and have ringed tails, but have lost these markings by the time they are a year old. There are twenty-nine sub-species, all of which are mainly diurnal, solitary and wide-ranging, from coniferous forests to semi-deserts in North and South America. They prey on deer, wild sheep and goat, beaver, various small mammals, ground birds, fish and large insects.
Characteristics: length of head and body 122–152 cm (48–60 in), tail 71 cm (28 in), weight 45.3–90.7 kg (100–200 lb)

TEMMINCK'S GOLDEN CAT
Felis temmincki

This beautiful cat is predominantly an animal of the mature forests, although it also extends into rocky terrains. It ranges from the Himalayas to south-east Asia, and preys on birds and mammals up to the size of small deer. Although this species is generally fox-red to gold-brown, some individuals are brown, black and grey. In China, a spotted variety resembles a leopard cat. When red and spotted Temminck's golden cat were crossed in Beijin Zoo, the offspring were all uniformly red.
Characteristics: length of head and body 78–89 cm (31–35 in), tail 48–74 cm (19–29 in), weight 6.3–11.3 kg (14–25 lb)

CHINESE DESERT CAT
Felis bieti

The Chinese desert cat is a medium-sized cat with faint, dark markings, a striped tail with a black tip and very hairy paws. Like the bay cat, little is known about the species but it is thought to be nocturnal, feed on rodents in bush and forested areas in the steppes and mountains in Central Asia.
Characteristics: length of head and body 76 cm (30 in), tail 30 cm (12 in), weight 5.4 kg (12 lb)

AFRICAN GOLDEN CAT
Felis aurata

The African Golden cat is about twice the size of its domestic relative, sturdily built with long legs, large paws, a small head and a long tail. It varies in colour from chestnut to silver grey. The cheeks, the inside of the legs and the underparts are white, and some have spots, usually on the belly and inner legs. It lives in high deciduous forests in west and central Africa, and is active mainly from dawn to dusk, feeding on rodents, small antelopes and game birds.
Characteristics: length of head and body 73 cm (29 in), tail 30 cm (12 in), weight 13.6–18.1 kg (30–40 lb)

CARACAL or CARACAL LYNX
Felis caracal

The only other lion-coloured cat in East Africa is the caracal. This solitary creature with its tasselled, expressive ears, has a spotted underside. Perhaps this is simply to camouflage the expanse of white belly; but it is equally likely that caracals, too, were once spotted, and their coloration has adapted to the more open habitat. The caracal is found in Africa and Asia in desert, savannah, scrub, and mountain ranges where it hunts birds, rodents, small ungulates and the fawns of their larger relatives. It is mainly nocturnal and terrestrial, although it is a good climber and jumper.
Characteristics: length of head and body 71 cm (28 in), tail 23 cm (9 in), weight 16.7 kg (37 lb)

JAGUARUNDI
Felis yagouaroundi

Often called the weasel cat, the jaguarundi with its elongated flat skull, compressed face, sinuous body and long tail, looks like a weasel or otter on long legs. The two colour phases, which regularly interbreed, are black to brownish-grey, and a chestnut-red. The eight sub-species range from southern states of North America to central South America. The jaguarundi lives in lowland forest and bush and, although it can climb, is mainly terrestrial. It sleeps in the middle of the day and hunts birds and small mammals through the rest of the day and night.

Characteristics: length of head and body 66 cm (26 in), tail 46 cm (18 in), weight 7.2 kg (16 lb)

JUNGLE CAT
Felis chaus

Thought to be one of the ancestors of the domestic cat, the jungle cat is sandy grey to tawny-red with black tips to the ears and tail. Kittens have tabby markings which fade as they attain adulthood. Despite the name, these cats live in woodlands, reed-beds, cornfields and near human habitations in northern Africa and Asia. They hunt both day and night for hares, birds, porcupines, frogs and snakes.

Characteristics: length of head and body 61–76 cm (24–30 in), tail 23–30 cm (9–12 in), weight 7.2–13.6 kg (16–30 lb)

FLAT-HEADED CAT
Felis planticeps

A very unusual feline, this is the only small cat which does not have fully retractable claws. It is about the size of a domestic cat but with a long body, short legs and tail, and a reddish-brown coat with white underparts. As indicated by its name, its head is broad and flattened with a ridge formed by its nasal bones. It has a pale band under its eyes and dark lines etch the cheeks. It is found in southern Asia, Sumatra and Borneo, usually in low-lying country near human habitation. It is terrestrial and eats frogs, fish and fruit, as well as being very partial to sweet potatoes.

Characteristics: length of head and body 56 cm (22 in), tail 18 cm (7 in), weight 6.8 kg (15 lb)

PALLAS'S CAT
Felis manul

The Pallas's cat's face is very similar to that of the lynx although it lacks ear tufts. It has a large body on short, stocky legs. Its coat is long and silky, and varies in colour from light grey to russet, with white tips to the hairs which give it a sparkling sheen. There are dark cheek lines, and the rings on its tail and its lips, chin and throat are white. It lives in central Asia, where rocky plateaux and river banks are its favourite habitat, and it hunts small mammals and birds mainly at night.

Scientists have hypothesized that the manul or Pallas's cat is an ancestor of the long-haired domestic breeds of today. This beautiful creature has a long, fluffy coat and ranges from the Caspian Sea to Tibet, and north to Siberia. The Caspian Sea forms part of the northern frontier of Iran, formerly called Persia; today's long-haired cats, often called Persians, probably originated in this area. But the layout of the manul's teeth, and the size and position of its ears are so unlike any domestic cat, that this hypothesis has since been ruled out. The most important difference of all, though, is in the structure of its eye. All domestic cats have a pupil which contracts to a vertical slit; in the manul it shrinks to a disc.

Characteristics: length of head and body 56 cm (22 in), tail 25 cm (10 in), weight 3.1–5.4 kg (7–12 lb)

SAND CAT
Felis margarita

A small cat with short limbs, a broad head and low-set ears. Its coat is sandy with light tabby bars on its limbs and flanks and it has a ringed tail. The sand cat frequents arid sandy regions in north Africa and south-west Asia. It is mainly nocturnal and hunts small rodents and reptiles.

Characteristics: length of head and body 51 cm (20 in), tail 30 cm (12 in), weight 2.2–2.7 kg (5–6 lb)

BAY CAT
Felis badia

Also known as the Borneo red cat, the Bay cat has a bright chestnut coat with slight spots on its underparts and limbs, and a few vestigial stripes on its chin. It lives in rocky areas in Borneo where it hunts small birds and rodents at night.

Characteristics: length of head and body 51 cm (20 in), tail 38 cm (15 in), weight 2.2 kg (5 lb)

RUSTY SPOTTED CAT
Felis rubiginosa

This very small cat lives in southern Asia. In India, it frequents scrubland, dried riverbeds and drainage systems near human dwelling, but in Sri Lanka it is found in forest and woodlands. It is nocturnal, preying on small birds and

mammals, and its fur is soft, short and grey, with a rufous tinge. It has spots on its paler underparts, white and dark streaks on its face, and the soles of its feet are black.
Characteristics: length of head and body 43 cm (17 in), tail 23 cm (9 in), weight 2.7–4 kg (6–9 lb)

BLACK-FOOTED CAT
Felis nigripes

The smallest of the African cats, possibly the smallest wild cat in the world, the black-footed cat is a sandy, ochre colour, lighter underneath with dark brown or black spots, streaked on its cheeks, throat, chest and belly and dark forelegs and haunches. It is a mainly nocturnal, ground-dwelling cat which hunts reptiles, small rodents and birds on the plains and grassy savannah of southern Africa.
Characteristics: length of head and body 36–46 cm (14–18 in), tail 18 cm (7 in), weight 1.8 kg (4 lb)

UNDISCOVERED WILD CATS

YUMA PUMA

In 1989, a male mountain lion or puma killed by a Native American along the lower Colorado River was brought in to the National Museum. Scientists thought the skull of the cat varied so considerably from others of its kind, they announced a new sub-species, the Yuma Puma, *Felis concolor browni*. The cat was described as smaller, paler and more yellow, with shorter hair and different skull measurements when compared with other races of the North American mountain lion. Between 1903 and 1929, three other 'Yuma Puma' specimens from the lower Colorado River found their way into the museum's collection. Two animals from northern Baja California and three from the Hualapal Mountains in western Arizona were subsequently added as well.

Recent research shows that the head measurements vary considerably, and that individual puma from the region travel so widely that it is difficult for the population to become sufficiently reproductively isolated for a separate sub-species to develop. Scientists now question whether the Yuma Puma exists as a separate entity. Since the Colorado River has been dammed, almost all of the wilderness areas where these pumas once roamed are now irrigated and have been turned into agricultural land. Today, only rare sightings of mountain lions and their tracks are made along the lower Colorado. But a thinly scattered population of mountain lions still exists in extreme south-eastern California and south-western Arizona. Convinced that its desert cats are 'Yuma Pumas', the Arizona Fish and Game department listed them as an endangered species and outlawed puma hunting in the Sonoran Desert. A desert mountain lion project has been set up and the mystery could soon be solved.

THE FABLED ONZA OF MEXICO

In the late 1980s, a large wild cat was shot on a ranch in Mexico. It was never properly identified, but local people believed that it was a mysterious, hitherto unknown species which they named the onza. Most scientists consider it to be a long-legged variety of the puma or mountain lion.

THE QUEST FOR THE BRITISH BIG CAT

There have been several recent reported sightings of large cats living wild in Britain. The Surrey puma and the Devon black panthers were reputed to be the size of a leopard, while others, like the Welsh ocelots, are slightly smaller. Many people are convinced of the existence of these outsized felids. Some claim they may be the same creature as the fabled 'Black Dog' and the 'Devil Hound' seen in past centuries. Others dismiss the stories and sightings as being the figment of fertile imaginations. No one knows for sure, but it is possible that some large unidentified wild cats are living quietly in the countryside waiting to be discovered.

OPPOSITE PAGE
A coat of one colour is the perfect camouflage against a uniform background of dry grasses. Jungle cats are as at home in reed beds, short grassland and arid scrub as they are in forested areas. Melanistic or black jungle cats are often found in Pakistan and India's dark jungles.

CAT COUNTRY

Wild cats are found in most areas of the world, the exceptions being the polar regions, Australasia and some island groups. The distribution of most species is today seriously diminished to the point where several species of cat could face extinction. People's greed for land has robbed the cats of their natural habitat and food sources. When forced by starvation into killing domestic stock, wild cats are killed as vermin. Fortunately, there are still some areas left where cats can roam freely. Their habitat can be varied or specific, depending on the adaptability and requirements of the individual species, and these factors are illustrated in this section.

OPPOSITE PAGE *The puma, also known as a cougar or mountain lion, is the most widely distributed of all America's cats. It ranges from Canada to South America in habitats as diverse as coniferous forests, tropical jungles, swamps, grasslands and scrubland, at elevations from sea level to 4,500 m (14,763 ft).*

Leopards tend to hunt in the cool of the early morning and late afternoon. During the rest of the day, they can often be found resting on a horizontal branch or in the crown of a tree.

The leopard is one of the most widely distributed members of the cat family. It is found throughout Africa, except in the Sahara Desert, as well as China, Siberia and in parts of the Middle East, Pakistan, India and south-east Asia. Its only requirements seem to be that there is sufficient food and adequate cover.

Jaguars live and hunt alone, females with cubs excepted. The cats are found in steamy jungles, savannahs and scrubby bush, where they need cover and a constant supply of water.

RIGHT *The otter-like jaguarundi is a wide-ranging species which lives in thorn thickets, dense forest and swampy grasslands. Its distribution extends from Texas in North America to east of the Andes Mountains and south into Argentina in South America.*

Pumas are as at home on the snow-covered plains of North as in the tropical rain forests and dry savannahs of Central and South America. In the cold north, they often hunt snowshoe hares, taking great bounds across the snowfields to catch them.

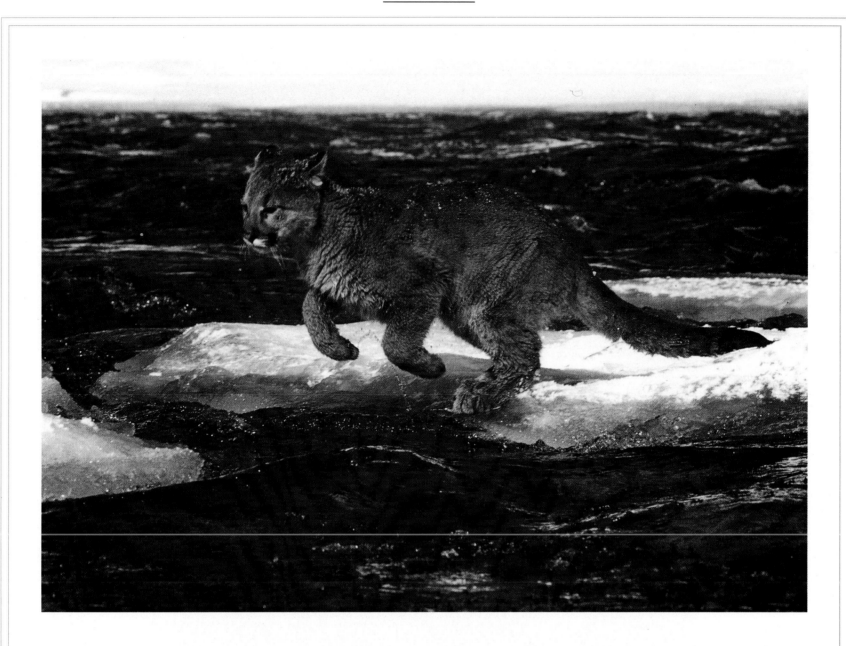

Pumas are not afraid of water. Those living in Canada and North America regularly swim across frozen rivers, although they prefer to leap from one solid patch of ice to another. They also venture onto the ice to hunt muskrat and beavers.

TOP *The jungle cat is one of the most widely distributed of all small cats, and lives in Europe, Asia and Africa. It frequents dense forests, but is also at home in swamps, arid bush, farmland and reedbeds.*

ABOVE *In Argentina, the pampas cat lives out in the open grasslands, but in other parts of its range, it inhabits forest and mountain ranges. Little is known about the species, but it is thought to be nocturnal and feed on small mammals and birds.*

LEFT *Although the fishing cat ranges through south west India and south east Asia, its distribution is patchy because it is restricted to areas of thick cover near water.*

The European wild cat inhabits coniferous and deciduous forests. It is highly secretive, rarely seen and difficult to study. It has a reputation for ferocity, but this is probably because it is usually encountered when cornered or trying to protect its young.

RIGHT Wild cats only give birth once a year, usually to two or three kittens, like this young European wild cat. The youngsters develop rapidly, hunting with their mother at twelve weeks old and reaching independence at about five months.

*Caracals hunt small antelope, rodents, birds and hyraxes mainly at
night. They rely on their large ears to detect the slightest sound
and use the tufts at the ear tips to reinforce facial expressions.
They flick their ears as a mild signal of threat.*

*The beautiful clouded leopard hunts at dawn and dusk in the
forests of southern Asia. Unlike most other cats, it drops down
on its prey from above, but like the big cats, stands
over its prey to feed.*

Tigers are most at home in forests, where their striped coats provide a perfect camouflage in the dappled shadows of the trees and grasses.

LEFT *Unlike most cats, which have a fear of deep water, tigers living in tropical areas spend a great deal of time actually in water. During the heat of the day, they often lounge in rivers to cool off.*

*Lions do not usually climb trees, but several prides in both Queen
Elizabeth Park in Uganda and Manyara Game Reserve in
Tanzania regularly do this. They lie sprawled over the lower
branches of favourite trees at midday, probably to escape the heat
and the biting flies. Since there appear to be obvious advantages,
no one known why other lions have not adopted the habit. It
could be that there are no suitable trees with low spreading
branches in other parts of Africa.*

The Spanish lynx is much smaller than its Eurasian relative with more heavily spotted coat. It is only found in southern Spain, in remote regions and the sand dunes of Coto Donana National Park, as well as a few isolated regions in Portugal.

The cheetah is the fastest animal on four legs. It uses cover to stalk its prey, but relies on high-speed sprints to catch its victims. This means it is confined to relatively open areas. Once cheetahs ranged throughout the dry plains and savannahs of Africa, the Arabian peninsula and Asia as far east as India. Today, their last strongholds are Kenya and Namibia. A few isolated populations remain in Asia.

RIGHT *An ocelot hunts either by laying in wait for victims or by slowly and quietly stalking round its territory. It stops as soon as it hears or sees prey and then relies on cover and its cryptically coloured coat to creep forward to within striking range.*

The rare snow leopard lives in the mountainous regions of Central Asia. It is generally found above the treeline at elevations of 2,700–6,000 m (8,000–19,700 ft), but during the winter it often descends to lower levels where prey is more plentiful. It is intolerant of human disturbance, and in the summer it moves back up to steep, rugged and remote regions.

*The Eurasian lynx is nearly twice as large as its Canadian relative.
Like this one, photographed in Germany's Bavarian forest, it
prefers forested areas with plenty of cover, but it can also live in
rocky areas and open bushland.*

ABOVE LEFT *The margay is one of the few truly arboreal cats. It hunts rodents, birds, reptiles and insects high in the trees, can descend head first down a tree trunk, and climb with almost the agility of a monkey.*

ABOVE RIGHT *In Africa, the golden cat is sometimes called the "leopard's brother" because they share the same habitat. The golden cat is much smaller than its so-called kin, and avoids competition by eating different prey.*

RIGHT *The little studied marbled cat is restricted to forest areas where it is believed to highly aboreal. Similar in appearance to the clouded leopard, its fur is softer and its undercoat thicker.*

The leopard cat is highly adaptable and thrives in a variety of habitats in China, India and south east Asia. It is nocturnal, swims well and hunts rodents, reptiles, birds and fish on the ground as well as in the trees.

About the size of a large domestic cat, the Andean cat lives in rocky terrain above the treeline in the Andes Mountains. Little is known about this species as only one or two wild individuals have been observed by scientists in the last one hundred years.

Bobcats range from Canada to Mexico, but due to the fur trade they have become increasingly rare. Montana, where this one was photographed, and northern Idaho are the last strongholds for the species which was once widespread in North America.

LEFT *The elegant, almost fox-like serval lives south of the Sahara Desert in Africa. It once lived in the Atlas Mountains of north Africa, but there have been no sightings in the region for over twenty years. This cat is rarely found far from a source of water and prefers well-watered grasslands.*

LIVING TOGETHER

With the exception of lions, cats are usually described as solitary, independent creatures. This section looks at cat society and reveals that cats actually spend more time together than most people imagine. Members of the opposite sex come together for the breeding season, and may stay together for several weeks before parting again. Females are rarely alone since they usually have cubs in tow, one litter dispersing often only when a new one has been born. Male cats spend more time alone than females, but young bachelors sometimes stay together until they reach adulthood. In the case of lions and cheetahs, they can team up for life.

OPPOSITE PAGE *Cheetah cubs are vulnerable to attack by lions, hyenas and birds of prey, and mortality is high during the first two months of life. Seeing a female with three sub-adult cubs usually only occurs where predators which threaten livestock have been eliminated, for example on ranchland.*

A female cheetah leads her cubs to a water hole for a drink.
Cheetah cubs start to follow their mother out on to the open plains
at about four months old, and they stay with her until they are
between fourteen and eighteen months old.

RIGHT *The king cheetah was once thought to be a separate
species, but it is now known to be a rare colour form. King
cheetahs are now being bred in zoos to ensure their survival.*

Servals, like most patterned cats, have prominent white "eye spots" on the back of their ears. These markings are thought to be used in aggressive displays, and may also help cubs to follow their mother in dark forests or thick undergrowth.

LEFT *The elegant, long-legged serval is strangely uncatlike in build. Looking more like a fox or maned wolf, its elongated limbs enable it to stalk rodents in the long grasslands of Africa where its prey is abundant.*

Male lions are driven from their natal pride when they are about
two years old. They usually leave with several brothers or
male cousins of the same age, and form a coalition which
often lasts for life.

LEFT *In wet areas, leopards drink regularly but they are not
dependent on a source of water, like tigers and jaguars. In the
Kalahari desert, for example, where water is not freely available,
they get all the moisture they need from their prey.*

ABOVE *Jaguars generally live alone, but during the breeding season, males and females can form a close if temporary bond. Mutual grooming is an important part of their courtship ritual.*

OPPOSITE ABOVE *Puma are solitary creatures, but immature siblings often groom one another.*

OPPOSITE BELOW *Male lions form close bonds with brothers or cousins. This enables them to hunt as a team while they are adolescent bachelors, and to challenge weaker or aging male lions in a pride when they reach their prime.*

Bobcats are solitary creatures, coming together only to breed. They are nocturnal and very secretive, so rarely seen. Like all cats, they are meticulous about keeping their coats clean. This is important as a matted coat is no longer waterproof.

RIGHT *The reign of male lions over a pride of lionesses can last as little as eighteen months or as long as ten years, depending on how successful they are at driving off unattached rivals on the lookout for potential mates.*

Pumas are solitary except for females with cubs. The young stay with their mothers until they are eighteen to twenty-four months old, during which time they learn all the skills necessary to lead an independent life.

Pumas live in a wide range of habitats from the cold north to steamy tropical regions. In warmer climes, they often cool off during the heat of the day by submerging themselves in the waters of a small river or stream.

Lynx are generally solitary, but sub-adult litter mates may stay together for a time after being deserted by their mother. This usually happens because she has given birth to a new litter.

RIGHT Most felids are solitary and the European wild cat is no exception. Very little is known about this species, but it is believed to be highly territorial with the sexes only coming together to breed. Dominant males usually avoid each other, but will fight when challenged by a rival of equal size and strength.

Adult male lions are the largest predators in Africa and considerably bigger than their mates. Although they rarely take part in a hunt, their superior size enables them to crowd out the lionesses at a kill and secure "the lion's share".

LEFT *Lions spend as much as twenty hours a day sleeping or resting. After a large meal, the pride retires to the shade of a tree and can spend up to four days resting while they digest their food.*

ABOVE *Unlike male lions, lionesses usually stay with their natal pride for life. Surrounded and supported by their family, they generally live longer than their male companions.*

OPPOSITE ABOVE *Tigers are essentially solitary cats, but in India they sometimes share a kill. They can usually only afford to do this where prey is abundant, and it probably only occurs between mates or related animals.*

OPPOSITE BELOW *Cats are sensuous creatures and often roll prevocatively. Unlike leopards, cheetahs are poor climbers, so they rest lying on the ground.*

Young leopards are playful creatures. Play serves to tone muscles for hunting. It also helps the young animals to perfect essential fighting skills in preparation for potential combat with rivals when they reach maturity.

*A male cheetah sprays urine on a prominent tree in his territory.
Scent marking informs other cheetahs that the area is occupied
and also imparts information on the sex and reproductive
condition of the owner.*

GROWING UP

The involvement of male wild cats in the progeny rarely extends beyond
courting and mating with the mother of their young. This is because it is an
advantage to both sexes to hold exclusive territories, and lead separate lives.
Females by comparison are diligent and caring guardians. Although they
spend their entire lives endlessly bearing and raising young, they never tire of
their duties and will risk death in defence of their offspring.
The photographs that follow illustrate the female's devotion to her babies – a
devotion which can last for periods of up to three years. There is also a look
at the exception to the general rule: the lion pride, where the males
participate in family life.

OPPOSITE PAGE *A lioness in oestrus mates as often as once every
twenty minutes, over periods of several hours, for up to four days.
Only about one in five matings results in successful fertilization.
For lions, sex is not only for procreation, and probably also serves
to reinforce bonds between lions and lionesses, allowing females
to mate with more than one male and reducing competition
between members of the pride.*

ABOVE *Female bobcats give birth in a secluded spot. For the first three months of life, the cubs – these ones are about a week old – are left behind in a hollow log, shallow cave or thicket, while their mother goes out hunting.*

OPPOSITE ABOVE *Snow leopards give birth to two or three cubs from April to June. These eleven-week-old cubs will already be following their mother on hunting expeditions.*

OPPOSITE BELOW *Snow leopard cubs are thought to accompany their mother until they are two years old. This nine-month-old individual still has much to learn before it can survive on its own.*

Like all cats, puma cubs are born blind and helpless and are totally dependent on their mother. Their eyes open at about two weeks old, but as early as the first week they will have staked a claim to one of their mother's teats. Exclusive rights to a particular teat seems to reduce competition among littermates.

*Leopards give birth in the most secluded spot in their territory,
where they are least likely to be found by baboons, lions, hyenas
and birds of prey, all of which are known to kill young cubs.*

Servals bear one to three kittens in a den usually in dense vegetation. The young develop rapidly, eating meat at about a month old, growing permanent teeth at six months, and reaching the size of their mother four weeks after that.

RIGHT *At three to four months of age, young cats, like this margay kitten, are ready to start following their mother on short expeditions in their immediate surroundings.*

Leopards, like all cats, carry young cubs by the scruff of their necks. Their offspring react by going limp, which eases the task of moving them to a new, safer location when necessary.

LEFT *Lionesses give birth in a secret location away from their pride. While their cubs are tiny, they keep them hidden from potential enemies like hyenas and unknown male lions, in a cave, burrow or thorny thicket. If they suspect that their hiding-place has been discovered, they will move the cubs one by one to a new and safer location.*

*The soft, spotted coats of young cats like these lynx cubs helps to
conceal them against a background of dense vegetation. This is
important because, for at least the first two months of their life,
their mother has to leave them for long periods to hunt.*

*A jaguar cub explores its surroundings. Young cats are inquisitive
and start to venture out of their lair or den at about six to eight
weeks old, although at this age they rarely wander far and are
ready to dive to safety at the first sign of danger.*

Young cheetahs lose the soft grey natal colouring, which helps to camouflage them, when they are about four months old. This coincides with the time that they leave the den area in which they were born and follow their mother out across the African plains.

LEFT Cheetahs give birth to up to five cubs, but in areas where the numbers of lions, hyenas and wild dogs are high, about 90 per cent of all cubs born die before they reach three months old. While her cubs are very young, female cheetahs rely on concealment to protect them in her absence.

Leopard cat kittens reach sexual maturity at eighteen months old.
Very little is known about the social behaviour of this species,
but it is at about this age that the young leave their mother
to lead a solitary existence.

RIGHT *After a gestation period of between eighty-six and ninety-*
three days, female clouded leopards bear between one
and five cubs, although the most common litter size is two. The
young suckle for five months and, like young tigers, males
seem to develop faster than their sisters.

Although male lions are known to kill the cubs of unrelated rivals, they are remarkably gentle and patient with their own offspring. They will tolerate having their manes and tails pulled much longer than females, and even allow a tiny cub to steal food from under their noses. Sometimes, however, they do lose their tempers and reprimand a cub.

*Lionesses are very patient with young cubs, even when they are
not their own. The pride females often nurse each other's
offspring, but since they are all related this has advantages. If a
mother dies, her relatives will continue to care for her orphans.*

THE HUNT

Wild cats are supreme predators and stand at the pinnacle of most food chains. Their principal hunting technique is to approach with stealth and caution, or lie in ambush for unsuspecting victims. They are highly adaptable, opportunist killers, and feed on a wide variety of prey. Any animal of reasonable size which comes within range is regarded as fair game.
The big cats are capable of killing prey much larger than themselves. Lions can bring down an adult buffalo or zebra; tigers regularly kill guar (a wild ox) where they are available; and leopards have been known to tackle a fully-grown eland weighing over (454 kg) 1,000 lb.

OPPOSITE PAGE *A tiger charges into a river in Ranthambhor, India after sambar that have gone there to drink.*

When stalking their prey, leopards keep a low profile, creeping
forward with their bellies often pressed to the ground. They try to
use all available cover, in order to get as close to their prey as
possible before launching an attack.

Tigers hunt using stalk and ambush techniques when they are hunting. They rely on their stripes to camouflage them among the linear shadows in the forest and long grass, as they stalk or lie in wait for prey.

During the winter, bobcats listen for mice moving about under the blanket of snow. When a mouse has been located, the cat pounces on the spot with both paws, trying to pin it to the ground, or to block off its escape route so it is forced above ground where it is easier to catch.

*A puma's preferred prey is deer but, when large game is scarce,
they will eat almost anything they can catch, including beaver,
marmots, mice, birds like this wild turkey, and even insects.*

Radio-collared jaguars in Belize were found to spend up to fifteen hours a day on the prowl. Their activity peaks are largely determined by their prey. In central America, where they feed largely on nocturnal species, jaguars hunt mainly at night. In Brazil they are active during the day and kill diurnal prey.

RIGHT *Unless a puma takes a snowshoe hare by surprise, its chances of making a successful kill are slim. While the hare is a light weight and equipped with wide, furry feet which enable it to skim over the surface of the snow, the puma sinks up to its elbows at every stride.*

Cheetahs use vantage-points like fallen trees, boulders or this termite mound to survey their surroundings. From this elevated position, they are able to keep a lookout for other predators as well as prey across the flat plains.

Able to reach sprinting speeds of 110 kph (68 mph), the cheetah is the fastest animal on four legs. However, they cannot sustain top speeds for long. Therefore they stalk their victims first so that they start the chase from as close as possible.

Female cheetahs help their cubs to perfect their hunting skills by
bringing them live prey, like this impala. The mother releases
the victim in front of her young, so that they learn to
kill for themselves

Young cheetahs leave their mother at about fourteen to eighteen months, but they stay and hunt together for a further six months. At first, young cheetahs are relatively poor hunters and kill hares, gazelle and baby springbok (above) which are relatively easy prey.

Leopard often haul their kill into a tree where they can store and eat it out of the grasp of scavengers like lions and hyenas. Some anthropologists believe that the early peoples living on Africa's savannahs supplemented their diet with meat stolen from leopards.

LEFT *Leopards have to stay alert at all times. They keep a lookout for lions and tigers which are potentially deadly enemies. They can do this most easily from a high branch.*

*In the dry season, lions often hunt round water holes, ambushing
potential prey visiting to quench their thirst.*

Lionesses are faster and more agile than the males and so do most of the hunting. However, the males are quick to seize the carcass.

In zoos, adult male lions need about 7 kg (16 lb) and lionesses 5 kg (11 lb) of meat a day. But in the wild, lions do not eat regular meals. Instead, they gorge themselves when prey is available to build up fat reserves for leaner times. A male lion can eat up to 23 kg (50 lb) of flesh at one sitting, which compares, weight for weight, with a man eating seventeen steaks for dinner.

LEFT *Lion cubs are always the last to eat. When prey is plentiful, they fare well, but when it is scarce, they are the first to suffer. As many as 80 per cent of cubs die, often of starvation, before they are two years old. However, if they all survived, Africa would soon be overrun with lions.*

*When their young are about one month old, female leopards start
to take small kills, like this dik dik, back to the lair.*

RIGHT *An ocelot's main prey is rodents and other small mammals,
but like most small cats, they are adaptable. They will include
birds, fish, land crabs and reptiles like this iguana, in their diet.*

WILD CATS AND MAN

Cats are supreme carnivores. They are the primary predator in many food chains and feed on a great variety of vertebrates. They have almost no enemies – apart, that is, from humans.

Due to their self-sufficient and independent nature, as well as their killing prowess, wild cats have for centuries been feared and revered, persecuted and threatened. Numerous myths and legends in most human cultures have grown around them. Today, many species are endangered because they continue to be slaughtered for their magnificent coats, or deprived of their natural habitat because it is destroyed by people.

OPPOSITE PAGE *Since the beginning of recorded time, cats have inspired and intrigued us – but sadly not enough to save them from persecution. All wild cats are threatened by habitat loss, many are still hunted as pests, and the coats of spotted species continue to be coveted by the fashion conscious. A few – like the Indian tiger with its reputation as man-eater – are feared so much that they have been hunted almost to exctinction.*

DOMESTIC CATS

Ten thousand years ago, primitive man began to cultivate plants for food, draw prolifically on cave walls and domesticate useful wild animals. We know that cats were among them as a few bones have been found in the ruins of old human cave sites. However, they are almost never found in the piled remains of hunted animals like deer, pigs and horses and this has led to the belief that they were not eaten. It is thought that, even in those early days, cats were probably encouraged round the camp fire and valued as pest-controllers.

All traces of the domestic felid then disappear from fossil records for the next 5,000 years, to re-emerge in Ancient Egypt. Evidence from surviving works of art of that time suggest that cats were kept as pampered pets and even worshipped as gods by the Egyptian people. No city granary was without a population of cats, and they were also used for hunting game. Mummified remains from the period indicate that the domestic cat descended from two main species; the jungle cat (*Felis chaus*) and the African wild cat (*Felis lybica*).

The cult of the cat started in Egypt where all cats, tame or wild, were treated with the utmost respect, to the extent that killing one could result in a death penalty. It is recorded that a Roman soldier who accidentally killed a cat in Egypt barely escaped being stoned by the gathering crowd. Subsequent fierce arguments over this affair are thought to have been a contributory factor to the war between Egypt and Rome.

The Egyptian regard for cats was even used tactically against them. During an invasion on the port of Peluse, an Egyptian stronghold, Cambyses, son of Cyrus the Great of Persia, is said to have included a live cat in the kits of all his front line soldiers. The battle ended in a bloodless victory for Cambyses, as the Egyptians preferred to surrender rather than risk killing a sacred cat.

The cat has been associated with Osiris, wife of the Lord of the underworld, as well as Pasht, the Lady of Life and the sister of the lion-headed goddess, Sekhemet. Pasht was a goddess of both the moon and the sun and represented the sacred eye of the god of light. Humans were sacrificed in her honour and the word 'puss' may have come from her name.

Domesticated cats were pampered excessively during the reign of the great cat goddesses. They were given choice titbits, comfortable beds, the best medicines money could buy, jewelled collars and their ears were even pierced and adorned with gold rings or gemmed studs. They were so revered that they were the first object saved in a fire. When a cat died, the whole family went into mourning and cut their hair as a sign of bereavement. The corpse was often embalmed, placed in a jewel inlaid coffin and taken to a cat cemetery for ritual burial. At the turn of this century, a particularly large feline burial ground at Beni Hassan in Egypt was uncovered when mechanical diggers started to excavate the area. As the soil, which was to be used as agricultural fertiliser, was dumped into the holds of waiting ships destined for Europe, it was found to contain an extraordinarily high proportion of bones. Researchers identified them as the remains of some 300,000 mummified cats and managed to save a proportion for future study.

During the cult of the cat in Egypt, export of these animals was strictly forbidden, but a considerable number were smuggled out by travelling monks and traders to Europe and the Orient. The Ancient Greeks, who thought highly of dogs,

valued cats merely as pest controllers, but the Romans pampered them as pets. Initially, their cats were a luxury for the wealthy, but they bred so prolifically that surplus kittens soon became available to the working classes. As the Roman armies advanced across Europe, they took their treasured cats with them and even named places after them. Caithness, in Scotland, means 'county of cats' and Kattewyk, in Holland, 'cat's town'. The first domestic cats to reach Britain were brought not by the Romans but by Phoenician merchants who traded them in exchange for Cornish tin.

Wherever and by whoever they were introduced, domestic cats prospered. They were valued as working animals but, just as we do today, ancient people found them endearing and respected them for their independence. The first law to protect cats was drawn up in AD 936 by Howell the Good, king of Wales. He set the penalty for killing or stealing a cat at the amount of grain needed to cover the entire animal when held by the tip of its tail with its head touching the ground. If grain was unavailable a ewe and her lamb would suffice. He also valued a newborn kitten at one penny, a sum which increased to four pence when it became independent of its mother and deemed capable of hunting alone. Every cat was expected to kill mice and the females to successfully rear kittens. Any animal which failed to meet these conditions could be returned to the breeder and either be exchanged for another kitten or for a third of the original price paid.

In AD 999, the first selective breeding programme for cats was drawn up by the then Emperor of Japan. He was apparently obsessed by some kittens born on the tenth day of the fifth moon which he isolated in his household in order to breed similar cats in the future. Japanese silkworm farmers of the time regarded cats as invaluable for controlling the mice which plagued their factories. But as other Japanese people followed the Emperor's lead, it became fashionable to own a cat as a status symbol and even parade one on a silk lead. Pet cats gained such popularity that there were soon few left to hunt in the silkworm factories which, as a result, rapidly became overrun with mice. Faced by a population explosion of rodents, the Japanese Government declared it illegal to keep cats as captive house pets, and the freed animals soon brought the numbers of vermin under control.

Throughout history, the cat has repeatedly proved invaluable as a pest-controller. As cities expanded, human waste accumulated and rats multiplied to the point where there were often more rats than people in urban areas. Rats became a significant pest but, more seriously, they carried flea-borne diseases, notably the Black Death. The outbreak of bubonic plague in London during 1660 originated from the bites of fleas living on the black rats which infested the sewers. Almost half the city's inhabitants died. Rat poisons had not been developed and traps were largely ineffective, so once again the cat was man's only ally. Ironically, cats were outlawed by the Church during the same period because they were often used in pagan ceremonies.

Whether cats were regarded as friend or foe, they rapidly spread worldwide. Few vessels sailed without cats as members of the crew because most insurance companies refused to cover rat damage without their presence. When the Crusaders returned from the Holy Wars, they brought back the first long-haired cats to Europe. These were probably eastern temple cats; the Persian variety with its thicker, silkier coat was not introduced until much later.

As people increasingly voyaged round the world, the cat travelled with them; unfortunately, the brown rat did so too. In the eighteenth century, this destructive and prolific rodent invaded Europe. Cats became a highly valued if not essential occupant of every house, office and store. Today, they are irrevocably established in human society, and are more popular than dogs as pets.

MYTHICAL AND MAGICAL CATS

For centuries, cats have been associated with witchcraft, pagan rituals and black magic. The alliance probably stems from the cat's hard, cold and often unblinking stare. Few people can look a lion or tiger straight in the eyes without experiencing a certain uneasiness. At the same time, their gaze can be almost hypnotic, so it is hardly surprising that they were regarded with superstition and mistrust. The colour and lustre of a cat's eyes is variable and their pupils can change from being large and round to narrow slits in seconds. The semi-precious stone known as 'Cat's Eye', and the 'cat's eyes' in the middle of the road which shine in the dark, are so called because they reflect the qualities of the eyes of their namesake. In the past, these characteristics, as well as the animal's reputation for inner vision, led to the use of cat's eyes in potions and charms. They were eaten as a cure for blindness and cataracts; the eyes of a black cat mixed with gall was believed to induce second sight; and tortoise-shell cats were thought to impart clairvoyant powers. The Chinese even believed that it was possible to tell the time by looking into a cat's eyes. This was because the size of the pupil was reputed to correspond with the position of the sun in the sky.

Cats were also believed to have healing powers. The dried and powdered liver of a cat was once used as a cure for gallstones. The Roman historian, Pliny, recommended cat's faeces mixed with mustard as a cure for head ulcers, and added it to resin and the oil of roses to encourage healing of uterine lesions.

Country folk used cats to forecast the weather. A cat which winked or washed behind its ears was a sign of rain; those which sat with their backs to the fire indicated a hard frost; and when they sharpened their claws on wood or behaved in a restless manner, gales were expected. In a Slavic myth, cats were said to be possessed by the devil during thunderstorms; angels said prayers with every thunder roll and aimed lightning at cats in order to cast Satan out. To avoid the risk of a lightning strike, cats were chased away from dwellings during storms.

Witches have long been associated with cats and numerous felines have been sacrificed to the Devil, but there were also instances where they were offered to God. In many cases, the unfortunate animals were burned and their screams were thought to be the anguished cries of demons. Cats were also kept as charms to bring good fortune, wealth and prosperity. The Chinese kept them collared and chained inside their stores; the older and more decrepit they were, the more luck they were believed to bring the shop-keepers. Their bodies were once plastered to the outer walls of houses to keep vermin and sometimes witches at bay. To this day, cats continue to be revered and respected because even the most domesticated maintain their independence and have a constant air of mystery.

MAN-EATERS

Instances of people falling victim to large felids are less common than press coverage often leads us to believe. Wild cats normally avoid contact with man but some do acquire a taste for human flesh. Tigers and lions are the most common 'man-eaters'. According to local papers, royal Bengal tigers have recently killed 500 people in the Sunarban mangrove forests of Bangladesh over a period of six months. Towards the end of the last century, two apparently healthy lions preyed regularly on the labourers working on the Uganda-Kenya railway. They killed more than thirty men in just over a year, and they terrorized the labour force to such an extent that construction work was halted until the lions had been shot. Leopards very occasionally adopt the habit. One particular Asian leopard claimed over one hundred victims before it was destroyed.

Man-eaters are usually old or disabled but there have been cases of healthy, young animals killing people. This may begin with an accident, a sudden close-encounter or cubs following the example of their mother. Some instances of this abnormal behaviour have resulted because of the extermination by man of the cat's natural food, and humans, being neither swift nor strong, are 'easy prey'.

THE LION PIT

The Romans capitalized on the lion's killing instincts, encouraging aggression by starving them, then throwing enemies, offenders and captives into a lion pit. The Romans are reputed to have imported more than 50,000 lions from Africa and Asia in order to enjoy this barbaric and popular spectator sport. This practice continued in Europe right up to medieval times.

PERSECUTED CATS

The black and gold skins of spotted and striped cats have been worn for centuries by Egyptian pharaohs, African tribal chiefs and important warriors. Highly prized for their symbolic value, their skins were thought to imbue the wearer with some of the qualitites of the cats themselves – their strength, cunning, grace and beauty. Tradition carefully regulated who wore and owned these skins, so the number of cats killed was relatively small. Then, in the 1920s, cats' skins, especially the spotted ones, became glamorous. For the following thirty years, tens of thousands of wild cats died an awful death, often in gin- or leg-hold traps, in the name of fashion. Finally, after long campaigns by many groups, the trade in these skins is now banned. But the illegal demand is still there, and many species are still losing ground to poachers and to expanding human populations. Small wild cats like the rare Geoffroy's cat, the ocelot, margay and leopard cat are particularly vulnerable because large numbers of pelts are required due to the intricate matching procedure required for each garment. When a species becomes too scarce to provide the minimum number of skins demanded by the trade, another more common one is exploited by the illegal hunters.

For too long, wild cats have been slaughtered simply because they are beautiful. Even today, there are people who think they can acquire some of the cat's grace and splendour by draping themselves in their fur. Thousands of magnificent cats die every year to feed this grotesque vanity. If we care, we can stop it by never wearing the fur of wild cats.

INDEX

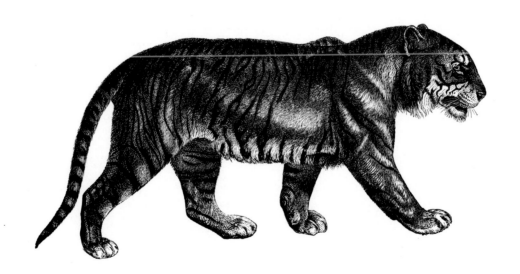